In memory of Bob Peteler and all those who
allowed me to be part of their final journey

JUST BE THERE

A GENTLE GUIDE FOR LIFE'S FINAL MOMENTS

Johanna Derbolowsky

Author's Note

This book is not a substitute for professional medical, psychological, legal, or spiritual advice. It is not intended to diagnose, treat, or offer specific solutions to end-of-life situations, but rather to offer perspective and compassionate presence for those supporting a loved one through the dying process.

Readers are encouraged to seek guidance from qualified hospice professionals, medical providers, counselors, and spiritual leaders when making decisions related to care and support.

The author and publisher disclaim any liability arising from the use or interpretation of the information within this book.

ISBN: *979-8-9928190-9-0* (*Paperback)*)
1st edition September 2025
Written by Johanna Derbolowsky
Copyright © 2025 All rights reserved.
https://quantumheartfield.com

FRQNCY MEDIA GROUP

Contents

Dear Reader

Thank you for picking up this book and allowing me to walk beside you during what may be a tender, emotional, and unfamiliar time.

Inside, you'll find practical guidance drawn from years of accompanying the dying and those who care for them. This book offers gentle direction when you don't know what to say, what to do, or how to simply be with someone at the end of their life.

You'll also find true stories that show how love, presence, and even silence can offer comfort when nothing else seems to help.

Your presence is the greatest gift you can give. Whether you're sitting quietly at a bedside, making difficult decisions, or actively helping someone to let go, you are making a difference.

And remember, during this time it's just as important to care for yourself, and to love and appreciate the gift that you are.

These pages are here for you, to help you stay grounded, calm, and connected, even when the path feels emotional or heavy.

With love and understanding,

Johanna Derbolowsky

CHAPTER 1

Presence

To be truly present in the moment means quieting the thoughts and opinions in our heads and simply being there. This isn't easy, especially when decisions must be made and emotions are running high. The mind wants to rush in all directions, and calming the mind is a true art. Yet even something as simple as a conscious, deep breath can work wonders. It helps soothe the mind and there is always time for one breath.

But to be fully present with another person requires even more, it requires that we listen. To do that we must let go of our own assumptions and judgments about what that person needs, wants or wishes. Only when our minds are clear can we truly listen.

Maybe you've noticed how people during conversations often start forming their response before you've finished your sentence. Their thoughts are elsewhere, and they only half-listen. Perhaps you've caught yourself doing the same. As soon as someone begins to speak, our minds tend to jump to conclusions, form judgments, and offer opinions. Truly listening is not easy. Sometimes we're so eager to share our own thoughts and knowledge that holding back feels like restraining a racehorse at the starting gate. And if someone needs more time to gather and express their thoughts, our minds can drift off to the many other things we feel we need to do. Rushing through conversations while only half-listening may seem efficient, but in truth, it steals from us the gift of real connection. The power of presence only reveals itself when we are wholly present.

As my mother grew older and needed more support from us and from professionals, she once said to me: "*The worst part is that everyone knows what's good for me and what I should do, but no one really listens to what I want or where I need help.*"

I was, of course, one of the people who thought they knew best and I already notice the same pattern with my own children. At times they are eager to tell me what I should or shouldn't do.

But when my mother said that, I listened. I realized I had no idea what it was like to walk in her shoes. I didn't know what it meant to be her age or live with her challenges. My advice came from a younger perspective and not from a place of understanding. That realization changed me. It allowed me to connect with others on a deeper level. Of course, I still catch myself being quick to judge, but I try to notice it and realign. What if we brought this level of presence to all of our interactions? It would be a beautiful gift and right now is the perfect time to begin.

At this very moment, your presence is needed. You have been given the opportunity to be fully present for someone as they embark on their final journey in this life.

CHAPTER 2

The Journey

Let's imagine for a moment that death is both the end of an adventure and the beginning of a new one. The only difference is that the life we are leaving behind is familiar, while the path ahead, the one the dying person is about to take, is a journey into the unknown. This is not your journey, it is theirs. Let them lead the way and choose how they want to prepare.

Before we set out on a trip, we make preparations. We pack what we need, take care of unfinished business, and make sure everything at home is in order. We want to leave with peace of mind. We make sure our pets will be housed and fed, our plants watered, our bills paid and the doors locked. And if others depend on us, children, a partner, or elderly parents, we try to ensure that they will be alright while we're gone. Ideally, we say our goodbyes with love and everyone wishes us well, so that we can leave with a light heart, open to whatever the new adventure may bring. But not all journeys begin this way, and not all farewells are filled with warmth or good wishes.

During one of my trips to Germany, I learned just how deeply a goodbye can affect the one who is leaving. That experience shaped the way I work with dying individuals and those they are leaving behind.

Homeward Bound

In my early twenties I moved from Germany to the United States. I built my life first in Maine, then in New York City, and later in Los Angeles. I still visit Germany about once a year. Years ago, when my parents got older, the good-byes at the end of my visits became more difficult. Every time I left Germany to go back to my new home in the US, the possibilities of it being the final goodbye felt stronger.

Of course, we never know what the future brings, and it is always possible that we are seeing someone for the last time. But as we, or someone around us gets older or weaker, we become more aware of how fragile and temporary life is.

This trip home was different for me. My oldest sister Sonja decided to accompany me on my train ride to the airport. At first, when I got up in the morning to go to the airport I felt the usual bittersweet energy of the goodbye. But my excitement to see my kids and return home always dispersed any sadness of leaving. I got up early to stop by the local market for my favorite foods. I picked up a delicious pretzel with butter and chives, local wild strawberries and some pastries to take on the plane, because as you know, calories don't count on flights. Food is simply a way to pass time.

I was packed, excited and ready to get home. Sonja and I had to take the train for an hour and a half to the airport. I had had a wonderful visit and was feeling good. As soon as we got on the train Sonja started crying. At first, I must admit, it felt nice that someone would miss me that much, but that feeling soon vanished. Her sobs grew more intense. She talked about being afraid we would never see each other again. She mentioned that our aging parents could die soon, and I would not see them again. Then it got worse, she even brought up the possibility of my plane crashing.

Each minute felt longer. My excitement to see my kids and get home faded. When we finally, in what seemed like an eternity, reached the airport, I was miserable and even a little afraid of flying. I had never been afraid of flying. Eventually we said goodbye. By then, I too was crying and nauseous. I spent my last few minutes calling my mom from the payphone near the gate. I told her I loved her and how important she was to me, just in case I would never see her again. I sat in my seat, exhausted and afraid. My pretzel and strawberries ended up in the trash. Even when I arrived my joy was overshadowed by exhaustion and a cloud of fear and dread.

I included this story because unfortunately, this is exactly what happens when someone embarks on the final journey of this life. The people who love them often make their departure more difficult than it needs to be.

When someone you love is dying, remember that this is their journey, not yours. Your role is to offer support, not to weigh them down with your fears or sorrow. They need your presence, your love, and your reassurance.

It is natural to feel grief and fear of loss, but those emotions should not become a burden for the one who is departing. Try to make their departure easier.

Peter

Peter came to me because his dear friend of many decades was in hospice, and he was preparing to visit him. Peter was unsure how to act and what to say. He didn't share his friend's belief about death. To Peter, it was simple, when we die, it's over. But his friend believed he was going home to his spirit family.

At first, Peter was hesitant about talking to me, because he knew I also believe in a continuum after death. But this wasn't about me, or even about Peter's beliefs. It was about his friend. In our short meeting I convinced Peter that his personal beliefs didn't matter, because he wasn't the one going through the dying process, or at least not now.

Whenever I meet with clients, I always ask the Divine to give me the right words. As soon as I did, the perfect example came to me.

I told Peter to imagine he was going to a retirement party and the guest of honor, the one retiring, was moving to Antarctica to play golf. Absurd, right? There are no golf courses in Antarctica. Everyone at the party thinks it's a terrible idea. But it's what he wants to do. It's what he has dreamt about doing.

I asked Peter: "*Would you go to his retirement party telling him and everyone else how stupid it is? Would you say 'this is ridiculous! Your adventure will be a freezing and miserable disaster'? Or would you wish him well and hope he finds what he is looking for?*"

Peter immediately got it.

A few days later, he called me to share his experience. He had walked into his friend's room and said: "*I am sad to see you go, but I truly hope you will find everything you're looking for in this next part of your journey. We both know I don't share your belief about spirit and the Divine, but that doesn't matter. I still hope for you, that it's everything you desire and even better.*"

Peter told me that by respecting his friend's beliefs and being honest about his own, without making it about himself, their friendship deepened. Their remaining visits were peaceful, meaningful, and even filled with laughter. Their final goodbye held an energy of love and respect.

Though Peter grieved the loss of his friend, he was at peace. He had been fully present, and because of that, he walked away with something truly precious. The memory of a beautiful, final goodbye.

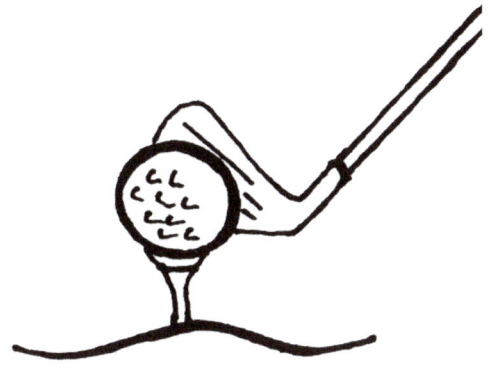

CHAPTER 3

Luggage

Just like any trip, the journey of dying comes with luggage. But not all of it belongs to the person who is leaving. We, as visitors, carry our own fears, worries, and unresolved emotions into the space, often unintentionally making their departure heavier than it needs to be.

Your Luggage

When you visit someone who is dying, you need to leave your luggage outside. Imagine packing your fears, needs, desires, beliefs, personal issues, and anything else that might weigh you down into a suitcase. Take a moment to check if you have really packed it all, every worry, every expectation, every piece of your own emotional baggage. When you are finished, set that suitcase down outside the door. It will be safe there. You can pick it up later if you choose. Take a few deep breaths before stepping inside.

Now, upon entering, you are fully present. You won't trip over your own emotions or anxieties because they are waiting outside. This is the time to focus on the person before you, the one who is preparing to leave this life. With an open and clear mind, you can listen to their thoughts, wishes, and fears. You can help lighten their load, rather than adding to it.

Their Luggage

Many people I have been with during their last days had worries about what or who they are leaving behind. Are the finances in order? Did I say everything I had to say? Did I make peace with someone who is still heavily on my mind? Did I forgive? Was I forgiven? These are all thoughts that weigh them down, like dragging a very heavy suitcase while hiking on a beautiful trail.

Tangible things like finances and belongings are of course the easiest to deal with. After my parents divorced my father remarried and had another family. When he was getting close to dying, his mind went constantly to his second family and the ones he was leaving behind. Will they be financially okay? Will they get along? Of course, he was not able to change any of those things anymore, but the worries still took up a lot of his thoughts.

During our many conversations, I kept saying, *"I will take care of it."* At the time, I didn't have enough money to rescue anyone, but I was sure that life would go on for those left behind and everyone would figure it out. He was able to relax and let that go, because I simply said "*I will take care of it.*"

When I've shared this story, some people have said, "*But that was a lie.*" It wasn't, because I had been sincere in my intention to do what I could. His fear wasn't about that moment, it was about the future. Neither of us could know what would happen. Therefore, my promise was exactly what it was meant to be: an honest intent.

I kept my promise and stayed in touch with his family. As for all the other promises, nobody became homeless, and everyone figured out their life.

I look at that in two ways. First, if you make a promise and have the ability to keep it, then keep it. Second, a promise can never be more than an intention to do something, because we never know what the future holds. If your intent is sincere, it is good enough.

The rest you can figure out later. Most likely, the dying person can't change the situation anymore anyway. It is just a thought that wreaks havoc in their mind and weighs them down.

However, if it is an immediate issue, try to resolve it quickly so you can say, "*It's taken care of*", to allow the person to release the burden.

With my father, once his practical burdens were eased, we could move on to the emotional ones. Looking back on his life, he saw many things he regretted and wanted forgiveness for. As a parent, spouse, coworker, client, or partner of any kind, there is always something that, in hindsight, we wish we had done better.

Helping a dying person let go is a gift for them and for you. Holding onto resentment only causes more pain and serves no purpose, especially at the end of life.'

Everything can be forgiven. It is your job to facilitate the process.

Many religions have some form of absolution, where a designated professional visits a person's deathbed, listens to their confession, and offers forgiveness. Religion has always understood how vital it is, not to carry unresolved guilt into the afterlife. Even people facing execution are usually offered a chance to receive absolution. It's a beautiful ritual.

But for some, it's not enough. They want to feel that they made things right, and are not just symbolically forgiven by a priest. Because you have left your own baggage outside the door, you can listen deeply, be present, and open for solutions to appear.

Here are a few suggestions for how you can help:

- Help write a letter.
- Organize a phone conversation.
- Arrange a visit, but make sure it won't create more tension or stress.
- If appropriate, ask a spiritual professional to visit.
- Become a messenger. Assure the dying person you will relay the messages and make sure apologies are delivered.

Good questions to ask are:

- What can I help you with?
- Is there something I can take care of for you?
- Is there someone you wish to see or speak with?
- Is there something that still weighs on your mind?

Sometimes, these things have already been taken care of, but they continue to feel unfinished in the person's mind. Reassuring them again and again that it's handled can be an immense relief.

Sophie

My friend's mother was in her late nineties when she passed away. She was ready to leave, and everything around her was peaceful. However, one thought kept resurfacing in her mind. Many years ago, someone very close to her had deeply hurt her. Although they had talked and forgiven each other long ago, a trace of that pain, or perhaps just the scar, still lingered. In her final days, the old wound unexpectedly resurfaced.

Fortunately, her loving daughter was by her side and gently asked, "Is this really what you want to carry with you?" In that moment, she realized that holding on to the past would only weigh her down. She took a deep breath, thanked her daughter, and let it go. A few hours later, she transitioned peacefully in her sleep.

It would be wonderful if we all had someone by our side to help us let go.

Many Eastern traditions believe that the things we are attached to, become the foundation of our next life. If that is true, then leaving this world in joy and peace becomes even more important. Regardless of whether you believe in reincarnation, religion, evolution, or nothing at all, one thing is certain: it is always better to leave a place in joy, love, and peace.

"If Death were to fall upon you today like lightning you must be ready to die without sadness or regret, without any residue of clinging for what is left behind. Remaining in recognition of the absolute view, you should leave this life like an eagle soaring up into the blue sky."
- Diego Khyertse Rinpoche

CHAPTER 4:

Guilt, Regrets and Standpoint

Life is not about failure or success, it is about living.

And yet, many people are burdened by guilt and regrets at the end of their lives. The wish, that they had done things differently, often clouds their view of reality. Guilt and regrets are tied to a specific moment in time, to something that happened at a certain point along the way. In that moment, we made choices based on who we were back then, on what we knew then, how we felt then, and the circumstances around us. But life goes on. We grow older, gain new insights, and see things with different eyes.

Suddenly, we're looking back at that moment from a new standpoint. The feelings we had back then are no longer present. The pressure or fear that shaped the moment is gone, and from where we are now, we wonder how we could have acted that way. But we forget that we have grown and changed. If we were truly transported back to that exact moment, with the same understanding, the same emotions, and the same conditions, we would likely make the same choice again. Because that's who we were then.

Our mind plays tricks on us. It tells us we should have regrets, because we should have known better, or done better, even when we truly did the best we could, from the standpoint we were at.

When a dying person suffers from guilt or regrets, it can be deeply healing to gently take them back to those moments. Then help them realize that they did the best they could with the knowledge, emotions, and circumstances at that time. You can also point out how much they have grown as a person since then.

Accepting the past as it truly was, opens the door to peace and to a peaceful transition.

CHAPTER 5

Transforming Regrets into Self-Love

Ask the dying person if there is anything they regret. If so, gently explore each memory with them. Invite them to remember the specific circumstances, the emotions, the pressures, and the choices they had at the time. Help them recognize that they acted from the understanding and resources available in that moment.

Regret often comes with the thought: "If only I had known then what I know now." The answer is simple: "You didn't know then and you did the best you could". This realization opens the way to self-forgiveness.

Once they've acknowledged the truth of the past, gently guide them back to the present. Show them how much they've learned and how far they've come. If anything still feels unresolved, it's not too late. Encourage them to find peace through an apology, a conversation, or simply by forgiving themselves.

Letting go of guilt brings peace. No one

goes through life without mistakes, and few people ever act with the intention to harm. When we believe that everyone does the best they can with what they know in the moment, self-compassion and love become not only possible, but probable.

John

John was carrying a heavy burden of guilt. When he was young, his girlfriend had poisoned herself, and he tried to save her. In a moment of panic, he called 911 and waited for help, instead of carrying her to the nearby hospital. But the emergency team came too late, and she died.

Many years later, as John lay in hospice, that memory surfaced again. He was overwhelmed with guilt and self-blame.

"*I should have known better. I should have done something different. It was my fault she died,*" he said.

I gently asked him, "*Did you want your girlfriend to die?*"

"*Of course not,*" he said, shocked at the question.

Then I invited him to take his mind back in time to that exact moment, when he came home from work and found her in distress.

"*What was going through your mind?*" I asked.

He described the panic, the fear, how he immediately called 911 and stayed by her side, trying to keep her awake and talking. He held her in his arms when help finally arrived, just as she took her last breath.

Then the self-blame started all over again.

"*I should've stayed on the phone and asked for instructions. I should've carried her down the stairs and run to the hospital. I should've done something else,*" he said.

I explained to him that he was looking at the same event from three very different standpoints in time.

First, the moment itself, when he acted instinctively and did what he thought was right.

Second, shortly after, when the help arrived too late, and grief and helplessness set in.

And finally, from the present, with all the knowledge and life experience he had gained since then.

I also reminded him that we can never know what else might have happened. Running to the hospital might not have saved her. He could have been hit by a car, or injured.

What we do know however, is that he did his best in that moment.

I asked him to see how much pain he had carried, not because of what happened, but because

of the guilt he held onto. Guilt over a decision that was entirely reasonable, given the situation. It had brought him a lifetime of suffering, but changed nothing about the past.
He nodded. Then I asked him to forgive himself, not for what he did back then, but for the pain he had caused himself all these years.

After our conversation something shifted in him. He felt lighter. We went on to explore a few more regrets, and each one softened as we revisited it in the same way.

John told me he wished he had forgiven himself sooner, but was grateful to finally let it go. In his final days, he welcomed visits from family and friends. He seemed much more at peace.

CHAPTER 6:

Gratitude and Things Left Unsaid

Unsaid apologies and regrets aren't the only things that can weigh on someone near the end of life. Sometimes, it's the good things, like words of love or gratitude that were never spoken, that can stay heavy on the heart. These missed moments can become just as burdensome as unresolved mistakes.

You have been given the gift of simply being present and listening. The quieter and more open you are, the more the dying person may feel safe to share what is truly on their mind. Let their words guide you and only offer support when it feels right.

I have sat with people who had a deep longing to express their gratitude to someone who had helped or loved them in the past. If this comes up, you can help. You might offer to make a phone call, write a letter, or even arrange a visit if possible. But always remember, this is their journey, not yours. Let their wishes lead.

If the person they want to reach has already

passed, there are still meaningful ways to offer support. You can help them write a letter and release it through a simple ritual, such as burning it, or speaking the message out loud together, imagining it being received. Moments like these often bring a deep sense of peace and completion.

Rolf

What stood out most about Rolf was his gratitude. No matter who did something for him, he always said thank you and made everyone feel appreciated.

When I was caring for him, not a single day passed without him telling me how grateful he was that I was there. Even when I did not cook his eggs to perfection, he was grateful. The next morning, however, he waited for me in the kitchen to show me exactly how he liked them. They were practically raw. After he slid his slimy eggs onto his plate, I proceeded to cook mine longer.

It wasn't my place to teach him how to be or what to like. My job was to be present with him, to give him space to open up, to let go of what needed releasing, and to help him have the best end-of-life experience possible.

Rolf didn't take to most of the nurses and

social workers who came to the house. Part of it was that he didn't think he needed them and wanted to manage things on his own. But it also had to do with how they spoke to him, usually telling him what he should do and how he should feel. I was thankful when they came by because it gave me a little time to myself. But he found their know-it-all attitude irritating. He endured the visits, but was glad when they left. That's when we would take a walk, and he would begin to share what was really on his mind.

Those moments reminded me again of how important it is to truly listen instead of thinking you already know what someone is going through.

Rolf had been a scientist, and he often challenged me to see things from different perspectives. He loved walking on the beach. One afternoon, while we sat at the shore, a few drones flew overhead. I've never liked drones. The idea of being watched from afar while trying to enjoy a quiet moment has always annoyed me. But Rolf appreciated them. He admired the scientific progress they represented, just as much as he enjoyed watching the dogs play on the beach.

When he became too weak to visit the beach, one particularly thoughtful nurse brought him a large box filled with sand from the shore. He placed his feet in it and imagined himself walking by the ocean. As always, he was moved by the gesture and full of gratitude.

After his wife passed, not long after their seventieth wedding anniversary, Rolf was heartbroken and disoriented. I sat with him as questions began to surface and waited quietly until he was ready to speak. He asked what I thought about death and slowly opened the door to a conversation about faith. It became clear that the Jewish tradition had always resonated with him. Together, we reached out to the local Rabbi for guidance and support. The conversations with the Rabbi comforted Rolf and helped him process his grief over the loss of his wife. I didn't try to convince him of my own beliefs. I simply listened and supported him in finding what was meaningful to him.

His wife had always been the one who kept their social connections alive. She cared about everyone, from close friends to the gardener. She organized, entertained, and radiated kindness. After she passed, Rolf had to find his own way to connect with the world.

And he did. In the last months of his life, he changed in ways that were incredible to witness. The once-reserved man who had kept his feelings to himself now sat on the couch and gently put his arm around the person next to him. He engaged in conversations with the gardener and welcomed those who visited. He showed more affection to his children and relatives than ever before.

It was amazing to watch his transformation. When his time came, he was surrounded by family. His last words were "*thank you*". Rolf inspired me. I hope that when my time comes, I will also leave with a grateful heart.

CHAPTER 7:

Laughter Is the Best Medicine

While you're helping a dying person release their emotional baggage, also try to bring in lightness and joy.

When we laugh, we are happy and we feel good. Even in moments of stress, laughter can bring light into the situation.

Conversations with someone preparing for death often revolve around what's still unfinished, like fears, or regrets. These are heavy topics that can weigh someone down. If possible, remind them of joyful memories, moments that made them laugh or feel good and share as many of those light, warm moments as you can.

That doesn't mean you should force jokes or turn on a comedy show, unless it's something they actually enjoy. What matters is that you get to enjoy heartfelt, genuine laughter.

Remembering fun experiences and the truly special moments in life can restore inner balance, especially when many of their thoughts are tied to pain or regret. If the person has spiritual beliefs, support them in focusing on the uplifting and joyful aspects of their belief.

Laughter eases the weight of the moment and the lighter we pack, the easier it is to travel.

Bob

When I met Bob, he had just purchased a black Scion FRS sports car at age 99 and renewed his driver's license. He had been friends with one of my clients, and we shared a daily lunch table together. Bob's wife and my client passed away just days apart. I was preparing to move back to Los Angeles but needed a few more weeks to take care of my client's affairs. During those days, I still went to lunch in the cafeteria and shared the table with Bob. He was full of life. His still-sharp mind craved adventure. We talked, and he soon found out that I did not really know Santa Barbara, even though I had lived there for more than six months. I had spent most of the time working. Bob saw this as a challenge. He was determined to make me fall in love with Santa Barbara.

I didn't know what to expect when he

asked me to meet him at 10 a.m. the next morning at the assisted living facility where he lived. I waited at the entrance, and he arrived on his scooter. He could barely walk and drove his scooter to his car, then slid easily into the driver's seat as if he were a young man. I was frozen in temporary shock, which gave way to fears about getting into his car. Internally, I was yelling at myself: Don't get into the car! I asked myself if I was crazy, but he was so excited, so I just got into the passenger seat.

I thought, or at least hoped, we were only going to drive a few blocks to the beach. As soon as Bob started the car, he told me how much he loved Santa Barbara, and off we went. The canyon road we were on had no crash barriers, and I was increasingly aware of the presence of death in the air. I don't mean his death; I was certain it was mine.

He was a good driver, better than many younger people, but my fear still grew. Then suddenly, I started to calm down. I told myself that Bob was not in charge of my fate. If this was the day that I die, so be it, and if it was not, I would survive. I tossed my fear out the window and enjoyed the scenery.

We drove past amazing vistas with views of the Channel Islands and the Santa Ynez

Mountains. Through mysterious-looking, foggy old oak forests, past grand mansions and avocado ranches. He showed me several houses he had built by hand over the years. We finally arrived at his friend's house for lunch. When she came to greet us, she looked at me and said, *"God, you are either brave or insane, I would have never gotten into that car."* Bob smiled and said, *"Yes, she is brave, but I noticed on the canyon road she was pale and probably thinking she was going to die."* He laughed like a little boy who had just played a good joke on someone.

That was the first of many outings. Just a couple of days later while driving, he noticed that he was a little low on energy and pulled over to let me take the wheel. Fortunately for me, he liked my driving. From that day on, he enjoyed relaxing in the passenger seat while I took us on daily adventures.

Every week we went further and visited places he hadn't been to in decades. He was full of tales and experiences spanning a century, and I enjoyed every moment.

During that time, I lived by myself in a small apartment not far from his place. Bob missed his wife, her companionship, and just watching TV together in the evening. I was new to the area and usually home alone at night, so I started coming over more and hanging out with him.

Bob had a great sense of humor, and we laughed a lot. He had no religion and was sure that on the day he died, everything would just be over. His motto was to enjoy life as much as possible.

Every morning when I entered his room, he had fewer things. He started giving things away and throwing out many of his photo albums. Bob wanted to leave this world the way he had entered it, without possessions. His affairs, Will and Testament were all in order. All that was left was some furniture, a few art pieces, books and trinkets, plus his coffee maker.

When he knew the end was coming, he was firm that there was no need to drag it out. He had asked his doctor if there was any medicine that would give him energy. The doctor, a young man, was trying to find the right words but finally said "*no.*" Bob didn't flinch. He just asked to be put on hospice. When the hospice worker came to meet with him later that day, Bob asked if the process could be sped up. The social worker offered the possibility of declining food, and Bob asked how long that would take. The answer was about three weeks. "*Is there a faster way, like assisted dying or anything?*" he asked, but the social worker said getting the approval for assisted dying would take longer than three weeks and the only faster choice would be to stop fluid intake. Bob again asked how long that would take, and the social worker answered, "*about three days.*" Bob smiled at me and said: "*I would love a glass of ice-cold water, but I am not having it anymore.*"

He had no interest in engaging with the hospice staff or talking about the past with them. That same day, he invited his close friends to stop by and said his goodbyes. He had left me a few of his photos, but I had to promise not to let anyone else get them. He didn't want to be held back by any ties or have someone perform rituals calling his spirit back, or some kind of Voodoo, even though he did not believe in it. He was making sure there were no ties left.

In the three days that followed, Bob first wanted me to get rid of all his belongings. He wanted the room to be empty. I did ask him for permission to leave the heavier furniture for later. I really did not want to deal with the whole moving-furniture ordeal. Luckily, he decided that when the time came, he would just turn his head toward the white wall and pretend everything was gone.

Hospice provided morphine to ease his last days, but after only one dose, he saw a rabbit run through the room. "*Oh no, they are trying to turn me into a druggie on my last days. I will not have that,*" he said, and with that, he refused all medication.

As we sat in the two remaining recliner chairs, he told me that there was no reason for me to waste my time with him anymore. He had loved my Quantum Heart Field coaching work and told me I should spend my time doing that, instead of sitting with a dying old man. I smiled and told him that since he was now too weak to kick me out, I was going to stay a bit. But I also asked him if he wanted me to leave because he wanted to be alone, or if it was because he thought it would be a waste of my time. He said that he enjoyed my being there but didn't want me to waste my time, so I stayed.

The evening that followed was filled with laughter. I told him my two very important rules:

"Bob," I said, *"there are two things I want to talk to you about. First, since nobody really knows what happens at the moment of death, please keep an open mind. If nothing happens and it is the end, so be it. But if for some reason anything happens, like you seeing a light, your wife appearing, or being pulled through a tunnel, just keep an open mind and go for it."*

He rolled his eyes a little, and I'm sure to humor me, he agreed.

"So, what's the other thing?" he asked.
"Well," I said, *"the other thing I need from you is a solid promise."*

He looked at me with curious eyes.

"If you find yourself as a spirit who can visit places, I want you to promise me that you do not come to my apartment and haunt the place. No turning on lights in the middle of the night or anything like that."

He burst out laughing. He laughed so hard his chair was shaking. When he could speak again, he said: *"I promise, even though that sounds like a lot of fun."* He had that cute sheepish grin on his face and the boyish sparkle in his eyes. I am sure he was contemplating how much fun that would be.

That night we both slept in the recliners.

The next morning, the hospice nurse helped him to his bed. He did not speak much anymore, and when he did, his voice was weak. I sat by his side silently, wiping his forehead and putting lotion on his dry hands. As he had wished, I helped him turn so he was facing a blank white wall. Occasionally, he would hold my hand, and there was a sacred silence in the room.

Bob was old-fashioned and very shy. He had always taken good care of his hygiene and got dressed without help. On the last day, his body got too weak, and the nurse had to help him to the bathroom. They did that with lovely respect, and I, of course, left the room to allow him his dignity.

I had a sense that he did not want me to see him die.

As Bob got closer to passing, I gave him a choice. About every two hours, I leaned over and informed him that I was going to get a coffee or something. I told him that if he wanted to slip out alone, it would be perfectly okay and that I loved him. If he wanted me to be present, I would be back in 20 minutes to be at his side.

Another time, I said I was getting lunch and would be gone for an hour, again letting him know he could choose what was best for him and that I loved him.

The assisted living place required a 24-hour caretaker to be in the room, and I had hired a nice lady to sit at the far end of the room in case he needed anything. She was, at his request, not to interfere or initiate any help. On one of those times I said goodbye, I stroked his hair, kissed his forehead, and left the room. I had barely reached my car when the caretaker called and told me that Bob had just taken his last breath.

She told me that he had put his hand on his forehead where I had moments before kissed him goodbye. When she walked over to see if he needed anything, she noticed that he was no longer breathing.

I had a sense that he was choosing to leave without me in the room, and I was grateful to have given him the privacy to do so.

What a beautiful way to leave this earth peaceful and quiet.

I am grateful to have been there with Bob. He was in life and death a great inspiration to me.

CHAPTER 8:

Everyone Is Different

I have been with many people in their final days. Some found comfort in the presence of loved ones, while others, like Bob, preferred solitude in their last moments. Often, those who are close to the dying feel a strong need to say goodbye. But it's important to remember that this moment belongs to the person who is passing, not to those who are staying behind.

Your role is to honor their wishes and create an atmosphere that is as peaceful and as free of stress as possible, even if that means limiting visits. This can be difficult, but it is essential. Your belief of what is best is secondary. What the dying person wants is what matters.

If you are with someone in their final moments, offer them the choice between dying in solitude or with someone they trust by their side.

This is their journey. Trust that they know how they need to go.

Mary's Farewell Celebration

Mary was someone who loved being around others. All her life, she enjoyed the company of family and friends. She knew everyone in her neighborhood, and later, when she moved into a nursing home, she embraced her new community with the same warmth. As her life came to an end, she invited many of her friends and family members to visit. She enjoyed telling them how much she appreciated their presence in her life. The nursing staff stayed on alert, ready to call her children, grandchildren, and great-grandchildren when they sensed the end was near.

Mary passed away in the arms of her daughter, surrounded by the people she loved, just as she had wished.

Not everyone chooses this path. Some prefer quiet solitude, others the company of loved ones. The greatest gift you can give is to respect their choice and support it in the best way you can.

Henry

Henry was in his early fifties and dying of cancer.

The pain had become unbearable, and he was ready to let go. His heartbroken wife and daughter begged him to keep fighting, hoping for just a little more time. But Henry knew it was over. He clung to life, day after day, hour after hour, unable to take that final step.

His wife barely left his side. She stayed with him almost around the clock, only stepping away when their daughter came to take over. Friends who visited gently encouraged her to give Henry permission and space to go, but his wife, Karen, insisted she had to be there when he passed. She feared she would never forgive herself if she wasn't.

After several days of this exhausting vigil, a nurse gently intervened. She explained that Henry might be holding on, because her constant presence was keeping him tethered. She encouraged Karen and her daughter to give Henry the space, both inward and outward, that he might need to let go.

Karen listened. She and her daughter spoke to Henry, who was barely conscious. They assured him it was okay to leave, and that they would find a way to go on. Karen added, "*If you want me to hold your hand, I will be back in an hour. But if you want to do this alone, I will give you that space now."*

They hugged him, kissed him, and left the room. Ten minutes later, when the nurse checked in, Henry had passed.

CHAPTER 9

A Last Visit

To visit or not to visit, this is a deeply personal decision, and it should belong to the one who is dying.

A dear friend of mine was nearing the end of his battle with cancer. I longed to see him one last time. We had shared decades of friendship, and I wanted him to know I was still there for him. By chance, I had business in his city the next day, so I called him. To my surprise, he answered the phone.

For a brief moment, it felt like old times, we laughed and shared memories. I told him I was in town and could come by, if he wanted. He thanked me and said, "*I know you would, but I want to leave it at this conversation. I don't want to see anyone anymore. I want you to remember me the way I was. It's been a great ride. No need for long goodbyes. Thanks for calling.*" That was the last time we spoke.

Of course, I was sad and grieving. But I was also grateful that I had respected his wish. It would have been easy to stop by the hospital anyway, but that would have been for me, not for him.

Not everyone gets to make that choice. One of my clients wasn't as fortunate. In his final days, some distant relatives decided to visit, despite his gentle request not to. His body was weak, and he was no longer the vibrant man they had known. Still, he found the strength to comfort them and thanked them for coming.

In our final phone call, he confided in me: *"I have so little time left in this body, and I wanted to use it to find my inner peace and not to be there for others. But they needed me, so I gave them what I could."*

Many people feel guilty if they don't make it to a loved one's bedside in time. They believe they have failed them. But this is a burden no one should carry. Just as birth is a profound, sometimes difficult and chaotic experience, so is death. Some people choose to go through this transition alone. The process can involve physical changes that feel too intimate to share, like the 'death rattle', the sounds of fluid building up in the lungs, or the body's final muscular release, which empties the bowel and bladder. Some people want to spare their loved ones from witnessing those final moments.

But beyond the physical, the end of life is often a time of deep inner reflection. And for many, that journey is best taken in solitude.

Before insisting on a visit, ask yourself:

Are you truly offering support or are you seeking comfort for yourself? It's ok to seek comfort for yourself, but not at the expense of another.

If you respect their wishes, you give them the dignity they deserve.

CHAPTER 10

When the Person Is Non-Verbal

If your person has dementia, is in a coma, or is no longer able to communicate verbally, it becomes even more important to be fully present. Just like in the chapter on "Baggage," take a moment to pack your emotions and personal concerns into a suitcase and leave it outside the door. Then take a deep breath and attune yourself completely to the person in front of you.

To create a sense of closeness and connection, a gentle touch, if welcome, can be helpful. Always let them know what you're about to do before touching them, adjusting their blankets, or making any changes in their space. An unexpected sensation can cause agitation or fear.

Imagine you are with a newborn baby. The baby doesn't understand your words, but it senses your emotions. If you're anxious, sad, or overwhelmed, the baby will feel it and become unsettled. It's the same with someone who can no longer speak. They can feel your inner state, and that's why it's so important to radiate peace, love, and a sense of safety.

As part of a hospital study on patients who couldn't speak, were unconscious or in a coma, my father administered acupuncture to see if he could better their situation. Because the patients were connected to monitors, he could see their reactions not just to the acupuncture but also to his presence. What he learned immediately was that patients became calmer when spoken to gently. People often raise their voices around non-verbal people, thinking it makes them hear better, but the monitors showed that a whisper close to the ear had an immediate calming effect.

If someone is breathing restlessly, you can help them by first matching your breath to theirs, then gradually slowing and deepening your own breath. They may follow your rhythm without even realizing it.

Music and reading aloud from favorite books or spiritual texts can also have a calming effect. A familiar song can stir memories, especially for those with dementia. It can transport them to a happy time and lift their spirits just like laughter.

Music can ease restlessness and, when it's sacred music, may deepen their connection to their faith.

I once knew an elderly woman with advanced dementia who had become completely disoriented. But when someone read her old poems, she would suddenly remember the words and recite them all the way to the end. Her mood would lighten, and she'd regain a sense of confidence. Those familiar poems became something she could hold on to, a source of comfort and orientation.

Find out what your person enjoys hearing. If you approach them calmly and are simply present, you'll notice what soothes them. Feelings and thoughts can find a way to get through even without words. When you offer peace and love, you receive peace and love in return.

CHAPTER 11:

Clark and the Power of Music

Clark was in the hospital, near death, and no longer speaking. There weren't enough staff members to spend time with the patients. I was a hospice volunteer at the time. When I entered his room, I noticed him trying to turn away from the television mounted above his bed. He seemed unsettled, moving his head from side to side. I introduced myself and asked if he'd like me to turn off the TV. He didn't respond, but his eyes kept drifting away from the screen. I followed my instinct and turned it off. Immediately, he became calmer.

I sat by his bed and gently moistened his dry lips with ice chips the nurse had given me. He was still restless. After a while, I quietly asked in my heart what he might need. In my short meditation the answer presented itself: music.

The nurse told me there was a CD player and a collection of CDs. This took place before streaming services. I tuned into his energy again and flipped through the CD folders.

Soon I found myself in the jazz and gospel section. When I came across Amazing Grace sung by Aretha Franklin, I just knew it was the right one. I grabbed it and a few more jazz CDs and returned to his room.

The moment Aretha's voice filled the room, his eyes softened, his breath slowed, and his whole body relaxed. He fell asleep. I let him rest and came back a few hours later. The nurse told me she hadn't seen him so peaceful in days. I kept moistening his lips and simply sat with him while the music played softly in the background.

Before I left for the night, I put Amazing Grace on again. A gentle, peaceful smile appeared on his face as he closed his eyes and drifted off to sleep once more.

Shortly after, during my drive home, the nurse called to let me know Clark had passed away. The music was still playing, filling the room with warmth as he made his final journey.

CHAPTER 12:

Fears at the End of Life

Some people are very afraid or just not ready to die, even when death is near. When I care for someone who is experiencing deep fear in their final days, I first try to understand the root of their fear. Is it caused by guilt or regret? By the feeling that something was left unfinished? Or by the belief that they didn't live well enough? Whatever the reason may be, I first support them in lightening that emotional burden just as I described in earlier chapters.

It is very helpful to find out what your loved one believes about death or possibly the afterlife. Then, see if there is something, books, films, or rituals, that aligns with their beliefs or worldview and could offer comfort.

I believe that what we encounter in death is exactly what we expect. Even as a child, I struggled with the Christian concept of heaven and hell. The idea that only people of a certain faith could enter heaven never felt right to me. I wondered how an all-powerful God could exclude someone from heaven just because they had never heard of Jesus, maybe because they lived in a remote rain forest or on a distant island. That kind of God never made sense to me.

Later, as a teenager, I became fascinated by Near-Death Experiences. I learned that people's descriptions of the afterlife were often shaped by their culture and beliefs, and reflected their traditional views. This curiosity eventually led me to study comparative religion, with a special focus on rituals and belief systems surrounding death and dying.

Many spiritual traditions offer support for the dying. They provide ways to prepare for the journey ahead, such as prayers for a peaceful transition, blessings for inner calm, or rites of absolution.

If someone is struggling with fear, especially if they believe in something like purgatory, you can help them shift their perspective. Help them forgive themselves. Encourage them to go toward the light, if they happen to see one. Assure them that love and peace are available to all.

In Tibetan Buddhism, prayers are recited for the deceased over several days to support their journey through the afterlife. These practices are described in *The Tibetan Book of the Dead*, an ancient text that is available in several translations.

If someone still cannot believe they are worthy of a place like heaven, despite all your efforts to offer comfort, you can still hold them in your heart and pray for them in your own way.

Jim

When I met Jim, he had already been ill and physically limited for many years. He was in constant pain, and our first goal was to ease his suffering. I used Quantum Heart Field shifting, a modality I developed to help my clients shift out of difficult situations into a new reality, along with mindfulness, and other healing techniques. The other goal was to help him prepare for his death.

He shared with me that a close relative had repeatedly told him that he was suffering because he had sinned and stopped going to church. In other words: *he deserved it.*

This belief not only deepened his pain but also added guilt and self-doubt, undermining every attempt at healing.

Over the next two years, we worked gently

and consistently to dissolve that belief.

It's not uncommon to ask, *"Why is this happening to me?"* or *"What did I do to deserve this?"* when life brings pain or loss. But life doesn't follow a clear cause-and-effect logic. One person might have a tragic accident, another might face a devastating illness without having done anything *"wrong."* At the same time, someone may commit terrible acts and still live a long, healthy and happy life.

Blaming oneself or others does not solve anything. Therefore, rather than searching for blame, it's more helpful to accept what's happening as part of life and shift the focus to the path forward. Questions like *"How do I face this challenge?"* *"What can I learn from it?"* and *"Where do I go from here?"* open the door to inner growth and peace.

To help Jim free himself from his guilt, I invited him to take a deeper look at the lives of others, both those he considered *'good'* and those he saw as *'bad'*. This helped him realize that suffering doesn't correlate with being a devout churchgoer or with moral worth.

Gradually, he was able to let go of the belief that his suffering was punishment for sin.

Still, a quiet fear of death and of purgatory remained. I encouraged him to explore videos on Near-Death Experiences (NDEs) on YouTube, so he could consider other possibilities beyond the one he had been taught. These videos gave him a new and more peaceful image of what might await him and with that, a growing sense of calm.

Jim and I worked on and off together for three years, connecting whenever he felt well enough to do so. During that time, he overcame most of his fears. In our final conversation, he was upbeat and ready to mentally support his fearful father, who was also close to dying. He told me he felt good about helping his dad prepare for a fearless death. A few days later Jim and his father passed away on the same day, only a couple of hours apart. Though they were in different locations, I am sure Jim accompanied his father.

Jim's story reminds us that in the end, it's about finding peace. Fear fades when we feel held, understood, and calm inside. Whether through loving presence, shared wisdom, or simply being there, we can help ease the fear of the dying.

CHAPTER 13:

This is Not the Time to Convert Anyone

Unfortunately, many people mean well but push too hard. They believe their religion holds the only truth and will 'save' the dying. Some even try to perform emergency baptisms. If the dying person asks for this, find a way to make it happen. But if they have a different belief, honor that. This is not the time to convince someone of your truth.

This is the time to bring comfort and unconditional presence. Find what brings your loved one peace and support them in their own way.

CHAPTER 14:

Books and Videos that Offer Comfort

In times of farewell, books can be loving companions. They can help make the unimaginable a little more tangible and offer hope, or the comforting feeling that we are not alone.

Here are some books I have found especially helpful and comforting:

Home with God:
In a Life That Never Ends
– *Neale Donald Walsch*

A heartfelt dialogue that explores the big questions of life and death, from the essence of our being and the meaning of life, to death as a transition into another dimension, and the question: What comes next?

The Afterlife of Billy Fingers:
How My Bad-Boy Brother Proved to Me
There's Life After Death – *Annie Kagan*

An extraordinary story of life after death,
told from the perspective of the deceased.
Touching and eye-opening.

Proof of Heaven: A Neurosurgeon's Journey into the Afterlife – *Dr. Eben Alexander*

A scientifically grounded and spiritually
uplifting account of a near-death experience by a respected neurosurgeon.

Life After Life: The Investigation of a
Phenomenon, the Survival of Bodily
Death – *Raymond A. Moody*

A classic on near-death experiences. A
powerful collection of personal stories that
explore what may lie beyond death.

Saved by the Light: The True Story of a
Man Who Died Twice and the Profound
Revelations He Received – *Dannion
Brinkley*

The autobiographical journey of a man

who experienced the afterlife twice and returned with moving insights.

Return from Tomorrow – *Dr. George G. Ritchie*

A deeply touching account of an extraordinary experience on the other side and the path back to life.

Videos

Documentaries can also help ease fear and open the heart to new understanding:

Near-Death Experiences – A documentary series by *Anthony Chene*

Sensitive interviews and fascinating near-death stories from around the world.

Everybody Dies, But Some Die and Come Back – A documentary series by *Elliot and Jesse Estrin*

Real-life stories of people who came face to face with death and returned changed.

The Tibetan Book of the Dead: A Way of Life – Narrated by *Leonard Cohen*

A profound look into the Tibetan Buddhist view of death and the soul's journey beyond.

CHAPTER 15

How to Handle Your Own Emotions

By now, you know that I encourage you to leave your personal issues outside the door and make this experience entirely about the person leaving this world. This is easier, when you're not emotionally involved. But what about when your feelings rise up, when old wounds start to ache, unresolved stories come back to haunt you, or waves of grief or anger take you by surprise?

If you feel overwhelmed, take a break, step outside, go to the bathroom, get a cup of tea, or simply breathe. When you're alone, acknowledge the feelings rising within you and find a way to release them. Go for a walk, rearrange furniture, or scream into a pillow.

What you resist will not only persist, it increases its power. Repressing your emotions will make them stronger and turn your visits into painful experiences for you and everyone involved.

Sometimes we just can't help it and old wrongs rear their angry heads like monsters wanting to strike just one last time. They whisper promises of satisfaction, but they never deliver. One thing I've learned is that the desire for revenge only fuels the fire, it keeps pain alive and drags it into the future. Grieving is much easier when you forgive.

Nisargadatta Maharaj says in the book I Am That:

"The memory of past unfulfilled desires traps energies, which manifest as a person. When its charge is exhausted, the person dies. Unfulfilled desires are carried over into the next birth. (...) I do not say that the same person is reborn. It dies, and it dies for good. But their memories remain along with their desires and fears. They supply the energy for the new person."

Michael

My best friend in high school, Michael, died in a car accident. Six months before his death, we had a terrible falling out and stopped speaking. I missed him deeply. We used to talk about everything, our fears, dreams, and beliefs. We had long philosophical conversations and comforted each other during hard times. In boarding school, far from home, he was my rock.

One morning I woke up and knew that the argument wasn't worth the loss. I called him that same day, and we talked for hours, clearing the air and laughing like old times. Michael had left the school, and we hadn't seen each other for months. On the phone, we made plans to meet during the upcoming holidays. I was so happy. I had my friend back.

I never saw Michael again. One week before our planned reunion, he died.

His death changed me. As a teenager, I thought I'd never get over the pain. But in time, the grief softened. What helped me most was that I had no regrets or lingering guilt. No *'I wish I had apologized'* or *'I wish we had made peace'*. We had already done that. We had forgiven each other. Today I don't remember what our argument was about. What remains is the love and the memory of a beautiful friendship.

If something or someone is weighing on your heart, don't wait, speak up and **forgive**. Let love be what remains.

Brenda

Brenda had mixed feelings about her ex-husband. They had raised three wonderful children together, but their marriage had often been rocky, and she had spent much of it feeling lonely. Their divorce was peaceful, and they stayed friends, yet some wounds had never fully healed.

When her ex-husband was nearing death, Brenda and their children visited him regularly. But she always made sure she was never alone with him. She knew he carried regrets about their marriage, especially about not being emotionally present, but she didn't want to hear them.

Deep down, she still held on to resentment. Whenever a conversation drifted too close to those unresolved feelings, she simply stepped outside. It was her way of being present without being overwhelmed.

After each visit, Brenda consciously worked to forgive him in her heart. With every step, she let go of the loneliness she had felt during their marriage and the moments she had wished had been different. And the more she released, the easier it became to stay in the room with him.

Eventually, they did talk about their shared past. She was able to accept his apologies and let go of her grudge. They agreed that those years were filled with learning and growth for both of them and had given them the wonderful gift of three beautiful children.

Through that process, Brenda brought peace not only to him, but to herself. Peace is not only a gift for the dying. It's a gift you give yourself. If something or someone is weighing on your heart, don't wait. Clear away misgivings, forgive, and let love be what remains.

CHAPTER 16

When Nothing Seems to Help

There are people who, at the end of life, are so trapped in physical pain that it seems as if they can no longer receive any kind of help. Also sometimes, you may reach a point where you simply can't bear to witness their suffering any longer.

Not everything you try will succeed. Please, do not blame yourself. In difficult times, it's essential to be your own best friend. Seek out comfort and support. Be there for yourself. Accept that some people are unreachable, don't want help, or can't accept it.

And never forget: even when nothing seems to work, what you're offering is still good. What you're doing still matters. Love and presence are powerful energies. Even if you feel your presence, your prayers, or your thoughts don't make a difference, know that love always finds its way. Even from a distance.

Uta

Uta's mother had been in the final stage of a serious cancer illness for some time. For years, their relationship had not been close. Thankfully, at the beginning of her illness, they had a few important conversations that brought them closer again. But they lived far away from each other and it was difficult to arrange visits, so they rarely saw one another.

One afternoon, Uta suddenly told her family, "I have to go visit my mom now." Her intuition told her to go see her mom and she listened. She got on a train and arrived well after midnight at the palliative care facility, where her mother was.

It was heartbreaking for her to see her mother restless, in great pain, and unresponsive. Even the gentlest touch seemed unbearable to her. Uta sat down beside the bed. She was simply there, present and willing to carry this final, heavy moment with her. Four hours later, the struggle ended. Her mom's face still tightened in pain as she took her last breath, before it finally relaxed.

Although they couldn't speak and there had been no final touch, Uta felt grateful that she had sensed the moment was near, had followed her instinct, and arrived in time. She was there, and her mother wasn't alone in her final hours.

A Mother's Pain

I met Megan years ago at a conference. She shared her story with me. Two years earlier, her 4-month-old son had been terminally ill. Toward the end, he screamed almost non-stop from the pain. Megan had been by his side for weeks and was completely exhausted. When his screaming grew even worse, something inside her gave out. She couldn't go back into his hospital room. She just couldn't take it anymore.

At the time, Megan was training with Dr. Jerry Jampolsky in Attitudinal Healing. She called him and asked for help. She told me she no longer remembered exactly how Jerry did it, but somehow, he helped her see her son's crying differently.

He told her that her baby's screams were like a kind of mourning song, a way to release pain. As adults, we forget how to express pain by just letting it out. After their conversation, Megan realized she too wanted to cry out like that. Jerry had helped her hear the screaming in a new way, and it allowed her to go back into the room and hold her son in her arms until his very last breath.

She told me that once she heard his screaming as a pain release and mourning song, she could bear it. She even found herself singing lullabies to him as she rocked him in her arms. Megan was so grateful that she was capable of handling these last moments with her baby.

Sometimes we encounter situations that feel insurmountable and seem to exceed our capabilities, that's when we need to ask for help. We are not alone. There are other people around us who can help and offer support. All we need to do is ask. I wish that nobody ever has to endure an experience like Megan, but whatever your experience is please know that you can reach out and get help.

CHAPTER 17

Bereavement

When you are deeply connected to some-one you love and find yourself over-whelmed by the fear of what life will be like without them, it can feel almost impossible to wish them a peaceful journey. It is the worst of heartbreaks, because it doesn't give the option of connecting again. At least not in this life. That is why you need to show up for yourself. Be your own best friend and find support for yourself. There are wonderful grief counselors, bereavement coaches and friends or family to lean on and ask for help. It is important that you take care of yourself, so that you have the inner strength to let your loved one go without placing any additional burdens on their path.

Grief is, at its core, our struggle to imag-ine life without the gifts we received from another, such as their love and presence. We became dependent on those gifts, and now we fear that the emptiness their departure leaves behind, will be too vast to bear.

But take a moment to remember: there was a time in your life before you knew this person, before you could even imagine the depth of love, or the depth of pain, that would one day come. So what happened? This person entered your life and expanded your heart. Your ability to love grew through knowing them, and your life was made richer.

When my children were born, I realized how suddenly my heart expanded. One moment I was living a good life, and the next, holding a tiny baby in my arms, my capacity for love exploded. From that day on, I couldn't imagine life without them. Objectively, I had a full and happy life before they were born. But I had become used to the love they brought me and to the love I was now capable of feeling.

The death of someone we love can bring immeasurable pain. My deepest sympathy is with all who have walked through such sorrow. And yet, I want to gently invite you to shift your focus for just a moment, to the gift you received through loving that person. How much more are you able to love now because they were part of your life?

Alfred Lord Tennyson wrote:

"Tis better to have loved and lost, than never to have loved at all."

When a loved one is approaching death, it is your time to offer them the gift of love and peace.

CHAPTER 18:

A Final Thought

There is no right way to support someone at the end of life. There is only your way, guided by love, by presence, and by doing the best you can at that moment. Being with someone at the end of their life is one of the greatest expressions of love. It is a moment of deep connection where words become less important than presence, and love speaks louder than anything else. As you walk this journey with someone, remember that you are not just witnessing an ending, you are part of a sacred transition.

Love is what remains and your love will find its way.

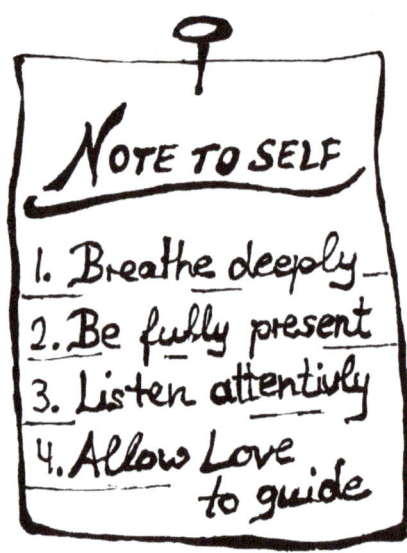

Reference List

If you find yourself in need of quick reminders of what to do:

- Leave your luggage outside
- Listen with your ears and your heart
- Listen to what the dying person wants
- Ask questions
- Lift worries and take away burdens
- Help change regrets into self-love
- Finish whatever tasks you can
- Hold hands
- Grant wishes
- Bring laughter
- Add Music
- Give a choice about dying alone or in company
- Wish them well for their journey
- Take away or lessen their fears
- If you don't know what to do ask a professional caretaker
- Hold them wrapped in your love like a mother holding a newborn baby

Being with a person at the end of their life is a privilege. It is a gift of healing, peace and love.

Acknowledgments

My heartfelt gratitude goes to the spirit of Robert G. Peteler, whose incredible presence and humor, even at the end of life, helped me write this book. Yes, Bob, you made it into one of my books just like you hoped.

To the Sabersky family, both those still living and the spirits of those who have moved on, and to Elsbeth Cram, who encouraged and supported me along the way.

To the spirit of my grandmother, who taught me at a young age that death is nothing to fear.

To my friends and family who allowed me to be there for them during their final days, thank you for trusting me with that sacred time.

And finally, to my patient publisher, Jody Colvard and FMG Press, thank you for putting up with me.

To learn more about Johanna's work,
teachings, and upcoming events, please visit
QuantumHeartField.com.

About the Author

Johanna Derbolowsky is a best-selling author, international keynote speaker, and healing and transformation coach. With her lifelong studies in the field of healing and her insights as a natural born clairvoyant, she has guided clients around the world through life's turning points and has helped them understand and shift the roots of emotional or physical pain. She supports people as they enter new chapters in life, career, relationships, and the sacred transition at the end of life.

As the developer of the Quantum Heart Field Experience, she helps people move from the consciousness of the problem into the consciousness of the solution.

Originally from Germany, Johanna has made her home in Southern California, where the ocean continues to inspire her daily life and work. She raised her children there and believes that life brings enough challenges. Her guiding intention is simple and steady: meet the world with kindness and make the path a little easier for others.